中國成語 现代用语

CHINESE PROVERBS FOR TODAY'S WORLD

Ariel Books

**Andrews McMeel
Publishing**

Kansas City

CHINESE PROVERBS

FOR TODAY'S WORLD

Emil William Chynn

ISBN: 0-7407-0510-5
Library of Congress Catalog Card Number: 99-65538

Calligraphy by Kuo York Chynn
Book designed by Junie Lee

Human Nature	23
Character	29
Animal Wisdom	37
Education	43
Family	49
Beauty	55
Health	59
Speech	65

FOREWORD

To be fond of learning is to
be near knowledge.
—*Confucius*

Growing up as a first-generation Chinese American, I was often struck by the fact that, for every occasion, my father would have a "Chinese proverb" at the ready. No matter whether I had gotten into a schoolyard fight, broken a window playing ball, or simply asked my father for general, worldly advice, the answer always came in proverbial form.

Not until later, probably high school, did I realize that having Confucius as a constant childhood companion was not the American norm. While watching *Kung Fu* on television, my American friends were most fascinated not by the unbelievable martial arts demonstrated by the hero, but by the mystical philosophy of his ancient Chinese teacher. It was all I could do not to say, "What's the big deal? That guy sounds just like my father!"

And not until years later, on my first visit to Asia during a medical school clerkship, did I first acknowledge that being brought up with Eastern philosophy could make me different from my Western peers. I was working at a hospital in Taiwan, explaining to the resident physician for the umpteenth time how, despite the fact that I *looked* "100 percent Chinese," I had grown up in an almost exclusively Caucasian town and so was really more American than Chinese.

"No," the doctor scolded, "you are not American. You will

always be Chinese. It's in your blood. I know you, and you think and act like a Chinese."

I was dumbstruck. Could it be that I had a Chinese brain in a Chinese body? Then I understood. All the hundreds and thousands of snippets of my father's wisdom had somehow sneaked in my ear and hidden within my skull, had taken residence and even helped

form the rugae and gyri of my complicated brain.

Sir Francis Bacon observed that "the genius, wit, and spirit of a nation are discovered in its proverbs." By recollecting the proverbs of my youth, I not only uncovered my own origins, but discovered a philosophy that was at once uniquely Eastern and poignantly universal.

This book reflects a cooperation between my father and myself that began unconsciously thirty years ago and was completed in a more structured fashion over the past three years. The aim of this book was not to give literal translations of Chinese proverbs, but to provide the English reader with a translation that sounds melodious but retains the original meaning.

前言

My father was charged with helping select from literally thousands of proverbs and carefully explaining the exact meaning of the original Chinese text. My job was to translate this into idiomatic English.

An example of this process is illustrative:

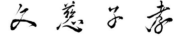

directly translates as "kind father pious son." Obviously, this is not even grammatical, much less idiomatic, in English. My father told me that the word for "kind" could also mean "loving," and the word for "pious" could also mean "dutiful." From this, the common translation is: "[A] loving father [makes a] dutiful son." Better, but not perfect.

I was seeking translations that, while accurate, would be catchy enough to sound idiomatic to the Western ear. This bias reflects my indebtedness to Chinese proverbs in my own development, and my resultant desire to make them more accessible to English speakers. After all, why go to the trouble to translate a proverb in such a way that it will never be accepted and adopted by the new language?

So, after some thought and dozens of permutations, I came up with: "Loving fathers make loyal sons." This version, I feel, retains enough of the original sense, while gaining a feeling of both meter and rhyme.

I hope our efforts meet with the reader's approval. Obviously,

in any translation, many possibili-
ties arise, and authors seem always
to be left pondering the road not
taken.

Emil William Chynn
New York, 1999

HUMAN NATURE

A room common to
many will be swept
by none.

■■

The best way to
avoid punishment
is to fear it.

What the eye does
not see the heart does
not mourn.

Patience in
one minute
of anger can
prevent one
hundred days
of sorrow.

Every smile
makes you a
day younger;
every sigh a
day older.

CHARACTER

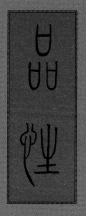

Rotten wood cannot
be carved.

■ ■

Men will despise
you only if you first
despise yourself.

When you paint a dragon, you paint his scales, not his bones; when you see a man, you see his face, not his heart.

31

Only a vessel
that is half-full
can be shaken.

Useless
as a youth,
useless
as a man.

34

Only distance tests
the strength
of horses; only time
reveals the hearts
of men.

ANIMAL WISDOM

He who
rides the
tiger finds it
difficult to
dismount.

Rabbits eat
not the grass
beside their
burrow.

Biting dogs
hide their fangs.

■ ■

The shrewd
rabbit digs
three holes.

EDUCATION

Learning that
does not daily
increase will
daily decrease.

One good teacher
outweighs a ton
of books.

■■

He who teaches me
for a day is my
father for life.

Only by
learning
do we discover
how ignorant
we are.

Learning is
like rowing upstream:
To not advance
is to fall back.

FAMILY

Easier to rule
a kingdom
than to run
a family.

Birds are born to fly
from the nest.

■■

Loving fathers make
loyal sons.

Easier to build
a wall around
one's house
than within it.

52

Your children
are like your
fingers; all
similar, but
no two alike.

BEAUTY

Hothouse
flowers wilt
where wildflowers
bloom.

Beautiful women
attract their fate.

■ ■

The beautiful bird
is the one
that is caged.

HEALTH

The wise doctor
never treats himself.

■ ■

Fit the cure to the
disease.

Blind men hear
what deaf men see.

■■

A quack needs no
scalpel to kill.

Hire a young
carpenter but
consult an
old physician.

Good advice,
like good medicine,
is hard to
swallow.

SPEECH

True words need no
shouting.

■ ■

Truth dribbles
out after wine
dribbles in.

Better to argue
with a wise man
than prattle
with a fool.

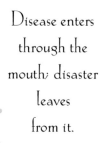

Disease enters
through the
mouth; disaster
leaves
from it.

Those living
near the temple
make fun
of the gods.

WIT AND WISDOM

When you go
outside, watch
the weather;
when you come
inside, watch
people's faces.

No needle is sharp at
both ends.

∎∎

Distant water cannot
put out a nearby fire.

Mend yourself before
mending others.

■ ■

Do no favors for
their rewards.

When drinking
water, remember its
source.

DEATH

死
亡

At birth we bring
nothing with us;
at death we take
nothing away.

Making one's bed
does not guarantee
getting up from it.

■■

There is but one
way to be born but a
hundred ways to die.

Life is but a
journey; death
is returning
home.